TISSINGT
& VIL

BRADWELL
BOOKS

Published by Bradwell Books

9 Orgreave Close Sheffield S13 9NP

Email: books@bradwellbooks.co.uk

British Library Cataloguing in Publication Data: a catalogue record for this boo
is available from the British Library.

1st Edition

ISBN: 9781909914926

Text by: Simona Sideri

Print: Gomer Press, Llandysul, Ceredigion SA44 4JL

Design by: Andrew Caffrey and typeset by: Mark Titterton

Photograph Credits: Mark Titterton and credited individually

Opening times

Tissington Village is open to visitors every day of the year. Visitors can arrive by foot, cycle or car and are most welcome to explore the village and surrounding countryside of the South Peak.

Tissington Hall is open to the public for 28 days each year in the summer although tours can be organized for societies and groups throughout the year.

These tours are led by local professional guides who can give a picture of the history and politics of the house over the last 500 years. And several times a year, Sir Richard leads private tours.

Times (between 10am and 7.30pm) can be arranged by mutual agreement. The minimum requirement is for 15 people but larger numbers are most welcome.

For dates, times and contact information, visit the website or email events@tissingtonhall.co.uk

www.tissingtonhall.co.uk

CONTENTS

INTRODUCTION AND WELCOME TO TISSINGTON HALL & VILLAGE

BY SIR RICHARD FITZHERBERT

Fiona and I welcome you to Tissington Hall, built by my ancestor Francis FitzHerbert in 1609 to replace the moated manor house to the north of the church. It has served our family as our main home for more than 400 years. We hope you enjoy your visit to Tissington and that you can explore the village and its businesses as well as the surrounding countryside on this and many more occasions.

Sir Richard and Lady FitzHerbert

"The beauty of Tissington, as with many an English village, is the result of evolution. No planner designed it: no bureaucrat decided how and where the houses were to be built. The village grew in an effortless and instinctive way that villages did in the days when the simplest unlettered cottar was possessed of an inborn taste and sense of rightness which is usually lacking even in the most sophisticated modern architect or designer." Robert Innes-Smith, 1986.

Tissington Estate is on the south edge of the glorious Peak District National Park, five miles north of the market town of Ashbourne in Derbyshire. It consists of just under 2,000 acres of rolling countryside around a picturesque village of 50 properties. At its centre stands the home that has been in the FitzHerbert family for over 400 years. Sir Richard, the current and 9th baronet, who inherited the title and Estate on the death of his uncle in 1989, lives here with his wife, Fiona, and family.

The Avenue, the main approach to the village

The by-road that leads to Tissington turns off the A515 between Ashbourne and Buxton to pass through large stone gate posts set beside a pretty lodge. From there, a stately avenue of limes leads, almost like a private drive, to the village. The trees were planted in 1971 by Sir John FitzHerbert, the 8th Baronet, to replace the Victorian avenue of lime trees that were felled because of decay.

The Estate includes several working farms, mostly farming beef cattle and sheep alongside one large dairy farm. The village is home and workplace to around 100 people, many of whom were born and bred here, like their ancestors before them.

Tissington Hall is open to visitors on 30 published days each year, when visitors can explore the splendid Jacobean mansion and admire the various extensions that were added over the centuries. The rooms are filled with paintings, furniture, art works and heirlooms collected by the family. Alongside the Hall there are ten acres of gardens including an arboretum and rose garden. The grounds are used to host various charity events throughout the summer.

The scenic and unspoilt village has plenty of attractions, including a Norman church and many well-preserved old buildings that house a variety of interesting and unusual shops and businesses. Including the very popular Herbert's tearoom and accommodation for those wishing to stay overnight.

There are six wells in the village that tradition says never dry out, even in the worst droughts. In thanks for this bounty of water, every year, on Ascension Day, the wells are 'dressed', or decorated, with large ornamental displays made of fresh flower petals. This colourful, ancient tradition is a sight worth seeing and people come from far and wide to enjoy the spectacle.

This guide book gives you all the information you need to get the best from your visit. We hope that you will enjoy your time in Tissington.

THE VILLAGE GREEN AND POND

Today, Tissington still looks as it did before the Industrial Revolution began to change the face of England. There are wide green spaces and the houses scattered about are unintentional and unselfconscious architectural gems. It is a rural idyll but one that has adapted to the times and offers plenty to charm and entertain the modern visitor.

A pretty lane, aptly called The Green, winds through the village. On the right it leads to the charming Duck Pond and beyond it to Tissington Trekking Centre, which offers escorted pony trekking and the chance to view some of Derbyshire's most stunning scenery.

Beside the Pond is Tissington Nursery. Housed in the Old Kitchen Gardens it is run by experienced gardener and plantswoman, Mairi Longdon, who grows many thousands of plants each year, including choice and hard to find varieties. "Our passion is plants and we pride ourselves in the quality and variety that we sell."

TOP: The Pond and the Kindergarten

Heading in the other direction, The Green skirts the wall of the churchyard. The church itself is at the top of a small hill and can just be glimpsed through the trees. Across The Green are several carefully maintained old buildings, including The Old School House.

There has been a school at Tissington since Queen Victoria's accession in 1837, when Miss Elizabeth FitzHerbert put up the money to build the School House. In 1995 it was renovated and became home to Tissington Kindergarten.

In the 19th century the village had a grocer, a shopkeeper, a shoemaker, a butcher, a blacksmith, a wheelwright and joiner, a stonemason, a carrier (who transported goods, sometimes called a carter) and a Mrs J.J. Murray who kept lodgings. The village was almost completely self-contained. Today the village remains a thriving community with a variety of businesses that help provide an income for its inhabitants.

TOP: The Village Hall and houses from the duck pond

HERBERT'S FINE ENGLISH TEAROOMS

Opposite the church is a beautifully converted old building that was once used to house carriages and cars. This is Herbert's Fine English Tearooms, the perfect place to relax with family and friends.

The scrumptious breakfasts and the delicious lunches from the Tissington Temptations board are definitely worth sampling. For a special occasion or a lovely treat, try the Sparkling Cream teas. Your welcome will be just as warm if all you want is a simple cup of tea and a slice of homemade cake.

The atmosphere is friendly and relaxed and the quirky décor and array of vintage crockery is sure to charm.

The Tearoom is available for hire for private parties and functions.

ABOVE: Visitors enjoying a break at Herbert's Fine English Tearooms

ST MARY'S CHURCH

To reach the church, follow the steep path, through the gate and under the shade of six gnarled old yews.

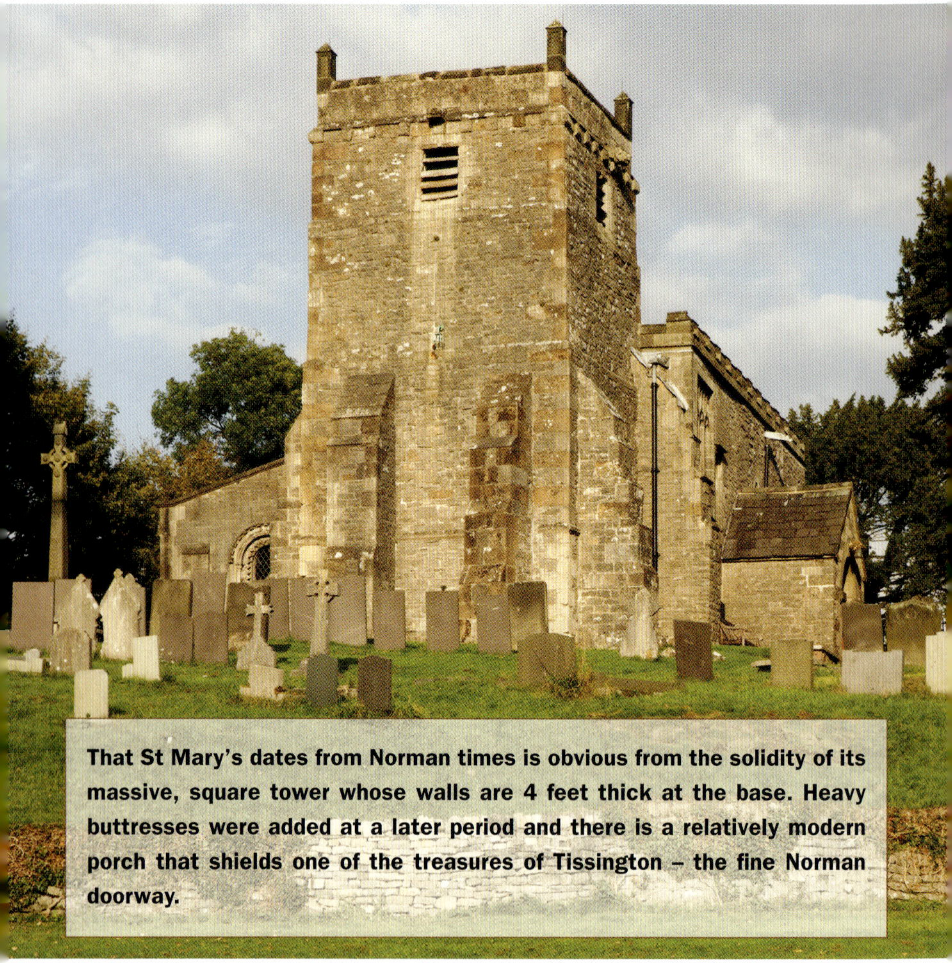

That St Mary's dates from Norman times is obvious from the solidity of its massive, square tower whose walls are 4 feet thick at the base. Heavy buttresses were added at a later period and there is a relatively modern porch that shields one of the treasures of Tissington – the fine Norman doorway.

Stop to take a close look at the door, especially the semi-circular stone arch around the tympanum. The workmanship is believed to be early Norman and is very well preserved for its age. Both side pillars of the doorway show a considerable amount of wear, commonly attributed to arrow sharpening. No doubt the stone pillars were very convenient for this purpose and it is known that archery practice on Sunday afternoons was very much encouraged.

Inside, the church is surprisingly compact and intimate as befits its origins as the chapel to the Hall (not the Hall we know nowadays but a building that stood here in former times). The plain, white walls beneath the dark timbers of the roof fill the nave with reflected light from the windows.

The simplicity of this space is somewhat disturbed by the encroachment, on the north side, of the elaborate Renaissance memorial in memory of Francis FitzHerbert, (died 1619) and his son John (died 1642). Highly ornate, this monument is expertly executed and provides a most interesting example of the costumes of the time.

However, the focal point of St. Mary's for the antiquarian must be the beautiful Norman font. It is ornamented on the outside with crudely carved and almost humorously drawn figures of men and beasts.

In the chancel, the Communion Rail is a feature. Scholars suggest it is the work of the Roileys of Burton and dates from between 1570 and 1580.

The church is open every day of the year between dawn and dusk.

LEFT: The Norman doorway with carved tympanum
RIGHT: The Nave looking east

TISSINGTON HALL

Built in Jacobean times, Tissington Hall is a particularly splendid specimen of its period. Like most old English houses, it bears the stamp of the centuries. A top floor was added around 1700 and, in 1780, the well-known Derby architect Joseph Pickford remodelled

the West Front. He added a hexagonal central bay and open arcading on the ground floor. The major extension of the Library and Billiard Room Wing was completed by the architect Arnold Mitchell in 1902.

THE FITZHERBERT FAMILY

The FitzHerberts came to England with William the Conqueror. They settled in Derbyshire where William FitzHerbert was granted the Manor of Norbury in 1125. In the 15th century, Nicholas FitzHerbert married the heiress Cicely Francis and so acquired ownership of Tissington.

The Hall was built by Francis FitzHerbert in 1609 and the FitzHerberts have lived there ever since. In 1784, George III conferred the baronetcy on William FitzHerbert for acting as Minister for Woods and Rivers and for his services as Gentleman Usher to the King.

RIGHT: This fine portrait of Sir William FitzHerbert 1st Baronet painted by Pompeo Batoni is located in the dining room

© Nick McCann

OPPOSITE PAGE: The Hall gate with ironwork by Robert Bakewell, with the main entrance in the background

The Hall is unique among country houses in that it faces directly onto the main village street. The façade is plain with upright mullion windows and a projecting porch. The arms of the FitzHerberts are carved in stone above the door.

A striking feature of the interior of the house is the Jacobean oak panelling in no less than 20 rooms. When Arnold Mitchell restored the house, in 1902, he was also asked to introduce a few modern conveniences (there was no plumbing and hot water was heated over a fire and then carried to the bedrooms). At that time most of the oak panelling was not visible. Revealed by the building work, it was restored to its former glory.

The furniture is of many periods, most notably from the era when the house was built. In the late 18th and early 19th centuries, Alleyne FitzHerbert, later Lord St Helens, was George III's ambassador to several European countries and he collected many of the fine objects you can see today.

THE MAIN HALL & DINING ROOM

The magnificent Main Hall is the largest and most impressive room in the building. It has a stone-flagged floor contemporary with the building of the house in 1609.

The wall panelling here was built in the 1750s and is decorated with intersecting arches topped with a deep dado and Gothic Revival arch motifs in plaster. The windows, too, reflect this taste.

© Nick McCann

ABOVE: The Main Hall

© Nick McCann

The main feature of the room is the stunning chimneypiece from the same period, with an overmantel in Hopton stone. The original receipt, dated June 17th 1757 hangs in a frame by the fireplace. Everything is carefully itemised on the bill, including the finials the Gothic head in the centre and a carriage charge listed as 'Carriage and boxes'.

The wonderful wood panelling in the Dining Room is typically Victorian: regular, dark and rather austere. It must be protected from the sun so the curtains are always kept shut.

This room was originally the kitchen before the extensions by Mitchell. The kitchen range was situated where the small fireplace is today, which seems barely adequate for such a large house.

The table is Regency mahogany by Gillow of Lancaster with a matching set of 13 chairs. As many as 24 guests can sit down to a meal here while the FitzHerbert ancestors gaze down from their portraits on the walls; for those wanting a unique dining experience, the room may be hired for private dinners.

ABOVE: The Dining Room

THE LIBRARY & STAIRWAY

The magnificent Library contains over 3000 books collected by the family over the years and was built by architect Arnold Mitchell along with the Billiard Room on the first floor.

Mitchell followed the Elizabethan custom of using plasterwork as wall decoration. The wonderful frieze, above the fireplace on the west wall, depicting a woodland scene of trees, birds and flowers was created for him by George Bankart, master of this art form.

Below the frieze is an antique convex mirror, a cunning device known as the butler's mirror often found in big houses. It is usually hung above the dining room sideboard so the butler could keep a discrete eye on the guests without them noticing.

© Nick McCann

ABOVE: The Library

The Library includes encyclopaedias, a set of Waverley novels and old Spectator omnibus albums. Many of the volumes carry bookplates of Lord St Helens and Sir Henry and Sir William, the 3rd and 4th Baronets.

A highly impressive and ornately carved Jacobean oak Stairway leads to the second floor.

On the first landing wall is the 18th century portrait of the handsome Richard FitzHerbert. On the opposite wall hang three framed documents bearing the seal of George III. They are the Ambassadors' credentials given to Lord St Helens to present to the heads of state of Spain and France; above the panelling are two large portraits of King George III and his Queen, Charlotte, commissioned by the King and given by His Majesty to the 1st Baronet's father. Identical paintings hang in the State Dining Room at Buckingham Palace.

ABOVE: The Stairway

EAST & WEST DRAWING ROOMS

The East Drawing Room was originally the Ballroom and is used today by Sir Richard and Lady FitzHerbert for private parties, charity functions and is also used to host civil marriages and civil partnerships. As in so many of the other rooms, it is the panelling on its walls that strikes you first. Where the wall panelling ends a decorative cornice runs along the ceiling, adding to the room's grandeur.

The room was created to feature shoulder high portraits, the main ones on show are: Lord St Helens as a young man by Angelica Kauffman and also in his ermine robes, those of a member of the House of Lords; a portrait of Lord St Helen's sister, Selina.

A large bay window looks south towards the church and the specimen trees planted by the current Baronet to recreate the ancient parkland.

© Nick McCann

The West Drawing Room is different from most of the other rooms of the Hall in that it has no wood panelling and it is covered instead in white wallpaper. This helps showcase the pictures, which include an interesting portrait of young William FitzHerbert from about 1760 that shows the boy with a cricket bat as if caught in the middle of a game. It was painted by Thomas Hudson, one of the most successful portraitists of the time who taught both Sir Joshua Reynolds and Joseph Wright of Derby.

There are several other family portraits around the room and a wonderful oak cabinet with many secret drawers.

ABOVE: The West Drawing Room
OPPOSITE: The East Drawing Room

THE TERRACE & GARDENS

The West Front was refaced in the 18th century in a rather severe classical style with a projecting Hexagonal Bay and open arcading on the ground floor. This was designed by Joseph Pickford a fashionable architect in the reign of King George and was intended as a kind of suntrap. The ladies could sit here after dinner and look out over the garden to watch the sun going down. In the garden below is a beautifully tended rose arbour, growing on what is said to be the most fertile part of the grounds. During World War II a great range of vegetables were grown here as part of the Land Army's effort to provide food for the country.

THE TRADITION OF WELL DRESSING

A BRIEF INTRODUCTION TO WELL DRESSING

Well Dressing is a tradition still practised in many Derbyshire and Staffordshire villages and is thought to be a custom dating from very early times. It is likely that wells were decked with offerings before Caesar's visit to England as part of pagan rituals to appease water gods and the spirits of wells. The ritual was later adopted by the Christian Church in a spirit of thanksgiving.

In Tissington some say the tradition started during the Black Death in the 14th century. Although the population round about was ravaged by the plague, in Tissington all survived. Their immunity was ascribed to the purity of the water from the six wells in the village. It became the custom to decorate the wells as a way of giving thanks and the tradition has continued ever since.

Whether it is true that Tissington's water saved its people from the Black Death or not, it is certainly the case that these wells have never been known to dry up, even in the most severe drought.

The dressing of the wells takes the form of creating elaborate tableaux with a biblical or topographical scene and a line from a well-known hymn. The decorations are made out of thousands of flower petals and other natural materials. It is a skilful art and the results are startlingly beautiful.

Boards are plastered in local clay, mixed with salt and trodden (like grapes) to the right consistency. The picture is traced onto the dry clay using a pointer or toothed wheel and marked out with the tiny alder cones or coffee beans. Flower petals are put in place individually; in such a way that they overlap like tiles on a roof so the rain will flow off the pictures.

The dressings are erected on the eve of Ascension Day ready for the ceremony of Blessing when the clergy process through the village to bless each well.

ABOVE: Making of 'Hands Well'

TOP LEFT: Hall Well TOP RIGHT: Blessing of the Wells, procession from the church
BOTTOM: Town Well OPPOSITE PAGE: Yew Tree Well

The six wells at Tissington are dressed every year with the Service of Blessing taking place on Ascension Day, a Thursday in May to early June every year. For details check the Tissington website www.tissingtonhall.co.uk

TOP: Yew Tree Well LEFT: A detail of a dressed well RIGHT: Coffin Well
OPPOSITE PAGE: Hands Well

THE GOOD SAMARITAN
20
13
LUKE CH10
VRS 25-37
REMEMBER THEIR BRAVERY
REMEMBER THEIR BRAVERY
'WHO IS MY NEIGHBOUR ?'
HANDS WELL.

SHOPS AND SMALL BUSINESSES

On a Wick and a Prayer Candle Shop

Annie Maudling and her team have been making and selling candles from the Old Blacksmiths' Forge for over 10 years. They offer an extensive range, including a host of scented candles. The shop is open regularly during the season.

☎ 01335 390639
www.onawick.co.uk

Tissington Trekking Centre

Run by Susan Torr the trekking centre caters for all abilities, offering escorted trekking and the chance to view some of Derbyshire's most stunning scenery.

☎ 01335 350276
www.tissingtontrekkingcentre.co.uk.

Edward & Vintage 1930s Sweet Emporium

Edward and Vintage is set in the former post office, offering a fine selection of locally handmade fudge, traditional sweets, chocolate and ice creams. Edward and Vintage is open 7 days a week from Easter until October.

☎ 01335 390537
www.edwardandvintage.co.uk

Bassettwood Farm

A farmhouse bed and breakfast with two double ensuite rooms, in addition there is a pretty shepherds hut and a bell tent. Delicious homemade cream teas are served every Thursday, Friday, Saturday and Sunday from 12-5pm; we are open all year.

☎ 01335 350866
www.bassettwood.co.uk

Overfield Farm

A lovely 17th century farmhouse that enjoys a unique position in the village, offering luxury B&B accommodation all year round.

☎ 01335 390285
www.overfieldfarm.co.uk

Tissington Nursery

With over 10 years of trading the former kitchen garden houses the nursery run by Mairi Longdon selling rare and unusual plants. A must for any garden enthusiast.

☎ 01335 390650
www.tissington-nursery.co.uk

The Old Slaughterhouse Butchery

☎ 01335 390300

The Estate Holiday Lets

Nurses Cottage(sleeps2)

Hoopers Barn(sleeps2)

Gardeners Cottage(sleeps 4).

All have wi fi, central heating, bath/shower and are furnished to a high specification. Available through the website.

www.tissingtonhall.co.uk

The Old Slaughterhouse

THE PERFECT WEDDING VENUE

EXCLUSIVELY YOURS...

© Steven Bradshaw

© red square photography

© Steven Bradshaw

© Photo Credit Ian Bursill

For over 10 years Tissington Hall has been opening its doors to couples looking for the perfect Derbyshire wedding venue. The beautiful stone-flagged Main Hall and the wood-panelled East Drawing Room are both licensed for civil ceremonies, alternatively many couples choose to get married in St Mary's Church and walk over to the Hall to continue their celebrations. The Hall and gardens provide a stunning location for photographs and drinks receptions throughout the spring, summer and autumn months. In 2012 the estate decided to enhance the experience that it was able to offer its guests with the addition of the Arboretum Pavilion, a stunning semi-permanent marquee set amongst mature cedar trees in the grounds. Brides and grooms have since been able to relish the opportunity to personalise the setting for their special day.

For more information about weddings at Tissington Hall please visit

www.tissingtonhall.co.uk/weddings